# FOR CHILDREN MAINLY

A. Jason Shirah

The Bethany Press
St. Louis, Missouri

Library of Congress Cataloging in Publication Data
Shirah, A Jason.
For children mainly.
1. Children's sermons.   I. Title.
BV4315.S526              252'.53                    79-26477

ISBN 0-8272-1010-8

Distributed in Canada by The G. R. Welch Company, Ltd.,
Toronto, Ontario, Canada

Printed in the United States of America

Dedicated to my own children:

Jane,<br>
Mary,<br>
Anne,<br>
Martha,

bright-eyed listeners in their childhood to many stories told by their father, and who from their birth have never known a loveless day.

# Contents

# Preface

During several years in the pastoral ministry I have included in the Sunday morning service of worship a feature entitled, "For Children Mainly." This has been provided with elementary children largely in mind. Children have a greater capacity for absorption of normal worship service happenings than adults usually accord them. Awareness of where they are is a significant possibility. The exposure to a climate of reverence is a process with cumulative effects, and this may be the most vital contribution that worship can make to a child.

The transmission of content, however, should not be forgotten. Efforts should be made by those who lead in worship to establish communication with the children. "For Children Mainly" has been my answer to such a need.

The use of the word "mainly," of course, implies that those beyond childhood are included in the communication effort as well. Some of the rewarding responses from congregations have been from adults who needed the point and who got the point.

I offer these fragments of thought for pastors, parents, and any other adults who may be interested, but even here they are "for children mainly."

A. Jason Shirah

# "Wouldn't You Be Lonesome Without Me?"

Family living is a wonderful thing. One of the best signs of the goodness of God is that we are able to live together as families.

We usually think that children are the ones who need their parents. The parents are independent; the children are dependent. There is truth in that. When children are little, their parents get up to see about them at night. When a child is too young to talk and when crying is the only way he or she can let somebody know that something is wrong, the mother and father try to figure out what hurts.

As children grow older, the parents are there trying to help them in their development until they are grown and leave home. Children need parents. The truth is, in addition to that, that parents need their children.

When our oldest daughter, Janie, was six years old, she and I took a little trip. I have done this with each of our four girls.

Janie and I left early one morning. It was well past noon when we got to a place where we could have our lunch. We went down a cafeteria line. She made her own selections of what she wanted. It was late, and she was hungry. She filled her tray, and I filled mine.

For a few minutes we ate and did not say much. Then she turned her little face up to me, and with the brightest smile she asked, "Wouldn't you be lonesome without me?"

I would have been very lonely without her. I needed her as much or more than she needed me. That has been so ever since.

You are important little people. You need your parents, but your parents need you too. You are not going to be a person someday; you are a person now. You are not going to be important someday; you are important now.

You can look at your parents and ask, "Wouldn't you be lonesome without me?"

# Sand Castles

Many children dread the end of the summer and the opening of school in the fall. One thing for which to be thankful, though, is that we can remember some of the good times that we had during the summer. Almost every family has had a vacation of some sort, and many of those were taken at the beach.

It is fun to ride the waves, if you are not out too far to make it dangerous, and to run and to play in the shallow water. It is a fun feeling to sit at the edge of the water and let the waves come running around you.

Often children and parents work together in building sand castles. It is hard to tell who has the better time. Walls are built with trenches around them. Towers go up on the corners. The main part of the castle is built inside with turrets on top and maybe a wall around the edge. Beach-loving families like to entertain themselves that way near the water.

There is one sad part about building sand castles. They don't last long. While the tide is out, children work and work. Finally, when the sun is going down, it is time to leave it all, take a shower, and get ready for supper. The next morning they go to the spot where the sand castle was, and where is it? It is gone. The tide has come in and washed it away.

Jesus told a story about sand and rock. He said that one man built his house on the sand. Another man built his house on a rock. A storm came and blew the house down that was built on the sand. The house that was built on the rock was hit by the same storm, but it stood. It stood because it was built on a good foundation. It was built on something solid.

Our lives are not to be like sand castles, built in an afternoon and washed away in the morning. They are not to be built on sand, quickly and thoughtlessly. They are to be built on solid rock, which is Jesus Christ. Then the storms cannot batter us down. We stand on him. Life stands on Jesus Christ.

# "I Spy"

One of the games that our children and I played when they were little girls is called "I Spy." Next door to our house in one community was a place called The Garden Center. It was a huge house where meetings and parties were held, and behind it was a lovely flower garden. The garden had benches placed in just the right spots for one to sit and enjoy the shrubs and blossoming flowers.

One child in particular enjoyed visiting The Garden Center with me. We would sit there and play "I Spy." I would say, "I spy something red." She would look all around to find the things that were red. She would make a guess or two, and then her eyes would fall on the huge, red brick chimneys of The Garden Center house.

"It's the chimney!" she would say. And she was right. Then she would spy something white, and I would guess and guess until my guesser was tired. I finally guessed a lovely, white, blooming water lily in the pool nearby, and that was right. It was fun for us to play "I Spy."

When you spy something, you look at it. Some people look at the world around them with appreciation and gladness. They spy a beautiful sunset or a lovely tree or a magnificent flower. Some are observant of things in a home, commenting on the paintings on the walls or the arrangement of flowers that the hostess had placed on the center of the dining room table at dinner. They spy the pretty things that make a home attractive.

In a little different sense, there are people who spy the good in other people. That is what they look for. Sensitive persons will spy pretty eyes or pretty teeth. They look for something good. They do that in thinking of the personalities of people as well. They see how kind or cheerful a person is. They look until they spy something good. It is always possible to find it.

# Finding Things in Clouds

Do you like to look at clouds? Some are bright and silvery. Others are dark and heavy. Clouds are very interesting, especially if you use your imagination when you look at them.

It is fun to try to find pictures in clouds. One may be shaped like an animal. You may see a dog or a cat or a lion. Another cloud may look like a face. Clouds can make one think of castles or the seashore. Clouds can look like trees and mountains.

People who are gifted paint pictures for others to enjoy. They paint people, animals, houses, the sea, flowers, woods, and mountains. Artists sell their paintings, helping them to live and providing enjoyment for others. People go to great buildings called galleries, where many paintings have been brought together, and look at the beautiful works of art. They never go out of style. They are good art. Some of the galleries do not charge admission. To visit others, one may have to pay.

When you lie on your back on cool grass, though, you can look up into God's great gallery and find the pictures that he has painted. They are big, and they are beautiful. And they are free! They are there for everybody who isn't too busy and who has a little imagination.

It is nice to know that God is thinking about us and that he shows us this in such interesting and beautiful ways. In showing us these things, maybe God wants to make a child's eyes dazzle with excitement. Perhaps he wishes to bring rest to the tired eyes of grown people. It could be that he thinks that somebody who has some talent will look at the art in the clouds and say, "I believe I will try to paint something beautiful myself." You may have done some drawing already. You may have done some pictures in watercolor. You may have talent in art. It won't hurt to try your hand to see.

10

# Tracks

Walk along the beach, and you may see the tracks of sea gulls. They are signs that these birds have been there resting, perhaps, or looking for food. People who enjoy relaxing in the woods are careful to observe the tracks of wildlife that they find there. Sometimes it is exciting to note that a deer has crossed a path or jumped a ditch.

A hunting dog that has been trained to do so can pick up the scent of animals or birds. Tracks also help tell where they have been.

In parts of the country where there is snow, it is easy to tell whether a person has recently crossed a field or yard by the freshness of the tracks.

The police look for tracks around buildings where a burglar has been. They have their own ways of going after people who do wrong things like that, and a track can help them know whether they have found the right person.

In a sense, all of us leave tracks. They are the tracks of influence. Those who come along later pick up knowledge about the people who have been there before them. Language, attitudes, and actions are tracks that tell those who study them what kind of persons we are or what kind of lives we have lived.

The world has many selfish and unkind people in it. They leave those tracks wherever they go. They think and plan and act for themselves. Nobody is as important to them as themselves. Those are the tracks they make.

Other people are kind and good. They say nice things to people and help them whenever they can. That is the kind of life they live. Those are the tracks they leave.

Sometimes persons do one thing or lead one kind of life, but they try to make it appear that they have done better than they have. That is called deception, and it is not a good way to live.

You can't always cover your tracks, so be careful what kind of tracks you make.

# God Thought to Make Our Pets

Having a pet can teach a child some things he or she needs to know. Some early lessons in responsibility come that way. The pet has to be fed, its bowls have to be washed, and it needs clean water regularly. To think about it when the weather is bad becomes a child's responsibility — when it is very cold or very hot or rainy. This is a good thought to think about your little animal friend, *It belongs to me, and I must be careful to see that it has what it needs.*

Pets are fun. They provide us with many happy times. Sometimes they can do cute things.

When I was a child, I had a fox terrier called Spots. He was white with black spots. His eyes were bright, and his little ears always looked as though he were expecting someone to say something to him.

Spots had lots of sense. He could sit up and fold his front paws in front of him. I taught him to climb a ladder to the roof of our back porch, and he seemed very proud of himself. When I would call him from the ground, he would tremble with fear at the thought of coming down that ladder. Finally he would put one paw on the top rung and start down. He was very slow and very careful, but eventually he would make it down. When he reached the ground, he would jump and run and leap on me as though he were saying, "I did it! I did it!"

Spots and I would go for long walks in the woods — just the two of us. I was happy with him, and he seemed to know that he was making me happy.

One day I noticed that something was wrong with him. He seemed in terrible pain. A cruel person had poisoned my little dog. The Bible tells us to be kind to one another. God means for us to be that way with people. Could he mean it about the way we treat animals also?

Our pets love us, and they like us to love them. We can try to keep them clean, healthy, and happy. God has given them to us. And so — let us be thankful to God for our pets and be kind to all animals as well as to all people.

# A Friendly Little Neighbor Named Will

Once upon a time, across from our house there lived a little boy named Will. When his family moved there, Will did not wait for the neighbors to come to see him. He went visiting the neighbors. I was his pastor, and so he felt a special freedom in coming to see us.

Will was a delightful little boy, full of life and conversation at all times. He always assumed that we had time for him when he came for a visit, which we usually did.

One afternoon Will came over. We had some guests, but that did not trouble him in the least. He sat down and entered into the conversation in a lively way. His mother, fearing that he might be staying too long, called and asked that my wife send him home. It so happened that only a few minutes before my wife had served us tea. Will was thirsty and drank half of his almost immediately. My wife told his mother that she would send Will home as soon as he finished his glass of tea. Will heard her, and it took him a full half hour to finish that drink! We were all amused and enjoyed his company.

Will made himself at home in that neighborhood. He was not only friendly with other children but with grown people as well. He was a sweet child and brought pleasure to everybody. I can remember his voice calling to me as I drove in from work.

Perhaps you could be in your neighborhood what Will was in ours, one who scatters brightness and cheer. Maybe there are adults without children or whose children are grown, whose lives would be gladdened by your happy face and voice. There may be older people, too weak and sick to get out much any more, whose days could be made better if you made them your friends.

Usually we think of adults taking time to be with children. It may be the other way around. They may need you the most.

# Adjusting to Changes You Have to Make

Several years ago our family moved from one town to another. Our children were all at home then, and the move to another town and another church did not appeal to them. They had their friends where we lived, and promotion for their father or not, they were not interested in moving.

But we packed and moved. They got into life in their new home. In about three weeks one of the girls said to her mother, "Don't tell my friends where we moved from, but I don't want to go back there. I like it better here!"

Grown-ups have adjustments to make, and so do children. It takes some doing to get used to change. When a family moves, for example, they not only have to pack up their things; they also have to pack up their minds. "I am going to do well and be happy in my new place," one must say.

Sometimes children have to adjust to a new school. You can stay alone, or you can get into the swing of things. Some activities you are included in by others; others you get into yourself.

You may move to a new neighborhood in the same city, and you must become acquainted. Making new friends among the children is not easy at times, but it is hard to be very happy without friends.

Some of you have had to adjust to a different church. Hopefully you have adjusted well. If you have, this has come about, perhaps, because of the help of members and teachers. It has come about because you have tried as well.

Help yourself adjust to change, and others will help you too.

# Not Everything That Hurts Is Bad

We usually think of pain as a bad thing. Anything that hurts is not good. A painless life would be wonderful, or so we think. We could well wish that some pain would go away. More than one person has wondered what good it does.

I want you to think this thought with me: Not everything that hurts is bad.

If you cut yourself or fall and skin your knee, it hurts. Your hurt finger or injured knee in hurting is saying to you, "Go tell Mama. Get something done for me." And so you do just that. Your mother washes the place that hurts, puts some medicine or a bandage on it, and before long you are playing again.

Pain develops in different parts of the body, and people to whom that happens either go to the emergency room of the hospital or get an appointment with a doctor. The pain has said, "There is something wrong. See a doctor." There are illnesses that come without pain, and they are to be dreaded because they come without warning. There is no pain to alert us to the fact that something is the matter with us. You can see, then, that pain is not bad when it lets us know that we are in danger.

Conscience helps us tell right from wrong. When we do wrong, conscience hurts us. Misery that comes from our having said something or done something ugly to another person is a good thing. When conscience hurts, it is saying that you have not treated your brother or sister or father or mother or friend right. It is your alarm system. The inward hurt is not your enemy; it is your friend.

A life that could not feel pain would be a life in very great danger. There would be no warning system. Life could destroy itself and not know what it was doing. To live too comfortably or too easily makes people soft.

Jesus suffered pain for those he loved. People have loved him for that. To suffer for others is hurt that is not bad.

# **Bridges**

One of my favorite places to relax is on a pier that juts out into a tidal river. It is a good place to sit and to think and to enjoy the marsh, particularly when the sun is setting. Everything is quiet and peaceful.

One day as I was gazing into the distance, my eyes fell upon a bridge joining an island to the mainland. Cars were on that bridge almost constantly taking people either home or to the city. That bridge is a necessary connector of those two bodies of land.

I began to think about the bridges in our lives that help us communicate with other people.

A handclasp is one of them. One person is introduced to another, and as a sign of their pleasure in meeting each other they shake hands. People who have known one another for a long time usually greet by shaking hands. It is a sign of warmth and shows friendship.

A handshake is a little out of place for you, and a grownup will usually put an arm around you when he or she greets you. That touch does it. You feel kindness and acceptance from that person.

A smile is a bridge between two people. When the muscles of the face relax and a smile sweeps across it, you know that all is well. A smile in return helps complete the building of that bridge of relationship. A person who passes us in a car, smiling and waving cheers us with friendliness.

Words can be destructive. They can sting, cut, destroy. They can break down bridges, separate persons from one another, cause others and ourselves much unhappiness. Words on the other hand can be bridges to help people share their respect and love for one another.

A gift can be a bridge. To purchase a present or to make something with one's own hands as a gift for another is enough to cheer that family member or friend.

Bridges on highways are necessary. We couldn't travel far without them. Bridges between people are among the world's best creations. Let's keep the ones we have and build more.

# Surprise, Surprise!

When a family or a group of friends wants to do something nice for a person without telling him or her beforehand, they may come to the door or come out with a gift or a cake, saying, "Surprise, surprise!" The person being honored will express delight that people have been thinking such nice thoughts and planning such an enjoyable event. It is good, as one person put it, to be "surprised by joy."

Life has surprises. They help to make good deposits in our memories of special occasions.

If people are creators of surprise, what about God? He is always doing something to surprise us with beauty and goodness.

Every morning when we wake up, God gives us the good news of life. Life is so precious that it is a fresh joy to awaken to it each day.

When we are riding in the open country, when we are in our yards or in a park or on the beach, we are surprised over and over again by the beauty of sunsets. "Look at the sky!" someone will say, and all eyes turn to it, sharing its colors and beauty.

Surprises are always coming to those who love the Bible and who read it with hungry hearts. There is so much good news in it. It happens sometimes when we read from the Bible that we see something there that we never knew was there, although we had read it before. A verse comes alive with meaning, surprising us with truth and encouragement.

So much has been done by people and by our good God to surprise us with gladness that we will do well to think about what we can do to bring that kind of excitement to other persons. It is a kind of repayment policy that never gets paid up, but it is fun to keep trying.

# Don't Play with Matches

"Don't play with matches!" All of you have heard that from your parents. Your mother and father know where danger lies, and they are right about that.

Matches are good in their place. They are necessary in starting a fire to cook supper if you and your family are campers. In the winter, matches help get a fire going in the fireplace. Matches are good for lighting candles on birthday cakes and for lighting candles in the church.

If people are careless with matches, however, they could set a house on fire. They could start a forest fire. Matches can cause loss of life and property when they are not used properly. Good in their place they are, but bad as playthings.

There are other things that are useful but also dangerous. We could not live without the sun, but it can cause us damage. Some sun is healthful. People like to get summer tans, but the sun can burn and blister as well.

Food is necessary and enjoyable. The call to dinner is good news. Appetites make us look at watches or clocks to see how long it will be until mealtime. But food can be damaging to the body if it is not varied enough and eaten in limited quantities.

Water is a good thing. We must have it to drink to live. Water in the ocean and in rivers carries great ships that transport food and machinery and oil that people need. Water can be dangerous, though, at the beach if a person gets out too far or in a pool if one cannot swim too well.

God's gifts are to be received with caution and care and thanksgiving. Almost every good thing can be abused. We need to think about what we do to spare ourselves and others unnecessary suffering through the misuse of God's gifts.

Back to those matches — they are not playthings. They are as handy as they can be in their place, but out of that place they are a "no no." We must keep ourselves from bad uses of good things.

# Life Is like a Raindrop

Life is like a raindrop. A raindrop is small but very important. You may have been outside at some time and felt a drop of rain. Then another touched your face, then another. Before long many raindrops were falling, and you would be inside looking out at a hard rain. That hard rain is made up of thousands of raindrops. Each is important for watering fields, flowers, and yards and cooling off hot city streets in the summertime.

One person's life may seem very small and at times unimportant to himself or herself. There are many people in the world. More than three billion people live on the earth. How could one person be important among so many?

The Bible tells us over and over how important each person is. God thinks that way about us. Jesus told us that the hairs of our heads are numbered. That was his way of saying that every person is very important in the sight of God. Every person's name and every person's hurt and every person's joy and every person's need is known to God. That is the way our heavenly Father thinks about us.

Think about how important persons are to one another. There are people who love you. Nobody else in the world can take your place in their hearts. Each child in a family is loved by that family in a special way. If one person is away on a visit, the family is lonely without him or her and glad when the time comes for that person to come home.

The church is made up of many persons — each like a raindrop. Every person in the church is important — children and adults. Many people would not know what to do without the friends and fellowship that they have as members of a congregation. They would be very lonely and unhappy. People in that kind of fellowship mean much to one another.

When you think about your life, think about the raindrop. It is made by God and serves its own purpose. If the raindrop could talk, it might say, "I am important to God and to people. Because of that, I am very happy!"

# Playing Make-believe

Playing make-believe is natural for a child. Baby dolls become real persons. They are made to do all kinds of things — open and close their eyes, cry, talk, and even walk. It doesn't take much imagination to think of them as real.

Children play house. They play store. They place police and doctor. When I was a child and there were passenger trains, we played train. Sometimes children may play church.

When I was a child, I would play church with my dogs and cats. I would round them up and place them before me, and then standing before them I would be the preacher. I am sorry to say that sometimes they did not pay very close attention! Sometimes they tried to leave before church was over, and I had to go get them and bring them back. This displeased them very much.

I would baptize my little animal friends even when they squirmed and tried to get away. My mother kept a little notebook in which I had listed the names of the animals that belonged to our family as members of my church.

"That is child's stuff," some adults would say, "nothing but make-believe."

Well, I played church when I was a child; but the older I became, the more seriously I thought about church. Instead of cats and dogs I began thinking of people. As I grew older I realized that God wanted me to be a minister. I believe that playing make-believe church was God's way of getting me ready for real church. How do you speak to a child except in a child's language? Make-believe was child's language, and there was more to it at the time than I knew.

The games you play do more than entertain you now. They are getting you ready for the future. Think about your games, because they just might prepare you to be that kind of person — a good person or a bad person; a person who loves peace or a person who loves violence; a person who respects other persons or one who does not care about them, or even one who is their enemy.

Attitudes are formed in persons very early. Your games help shape your thoughts and your future. Healthy games help make a wholesome life.

# Save Your Letters

Since I was a child, I have enjoyed saving my letters. My father died when I was ten years old, and I have some letters that he wrote me when I was young. I did not know when I saved them how much I would treasure them in later years.

I have stacks of letters that my mother and other members of my family wrote to me during my years in college. As I look back on those days, I am glad I kept them.

During my years in the ministry I have had some wonderful friends with whom I have carried on a correspondence. I have saved those letters as well.

My wife and daughters have written me many times when I was away from home. They have given me sweet cards on special occasions, such as birthdays and Father's Day, and I have them all. I would not part with them for anything.

To read those letters now refreshes my mind with the love that I have had for those people and the affection that they have had for me. They remind me of my good fortune in having the family that I have, the good home in which I was reared, and the friendships that I have enjoyed. Special times and seasons are brought clearly to mind again as I reread those letters that made me so happy when I first received them.

You are too young to have gotten very many letters or cards like that, but as you grow older you will receive them. I want to suggest that you find a place among your things to keep them. It will help you know how much other people love you. To have that love is wonderful, and to be able to be reminded of it as the years pass will do you good. If you do that, you will be able to say, "I remember, and I'm glad."

# You Are Part of a Big Family

Families vary in size. Some children have one parent and others two. Some parents have only one child, and others have two, three, four, five, six — and a few, even more. So, we would say that some of us live in small families and others in medium-sized and others in large families.

There is another family of which you are a part that is very large. That family is called the church. Another name for a family is a household. Paul in the New Testament talked about the "household of faith" (Gal. 6:10) and the "household of God" (Eph. 2:19). He could easily have said the "family of faith" and the "family of God."

It is good to think of the church as a household or as a family. God is our Father. He is the provider. He is interested in having all of the needs of his family supplied. We are the children who look to the Father for our very life. We have food and clothing and beauty because he provides them. Birth and growth and health and contentment and joy all come from him.

God, our Father, helps us find out what we are to do and what we are to be. In this family with God as our Father we have many brothers and sisters. All of the people who make up the church are that.

In this big church family there is a lot of love. Many, many people share the joy of others when they are happy. They help them bear their sorrows when they are sad. Grown people help teach the children the truth of God, and children make the grown people think with many of their loving ways and kind, thoughtful acts.

The wonderful thing about belonging to the family of the church is that people never have to leave home. They can be in it all their lives. Wherever they go there are other Christians, and there is a church, and they can meet new members of this wonderful, big family.

So, you see, you belong to two families, the one where you live at home and the church. When we say our prayers, we can thank God for these blessings that make us so happy.

22

# The Meaning of Your Name

Long ago in Bible times many people's names were supposed to describe strong features of their characters. "Zillah" meant "shady." Perhaps she was supposed to keep her cool better than others. "Gad" meant "fortunate." "Orpah" meant "freshness of youth." "John" meant "one whom God loves." "Barnabas" meant "son of encouragement."

Our names do not have meanings such as that. Our parents selected our names because they belonged to other family members for whom they wished to name us or simply because they thought those names were pretty ones.

Even so, our names can stand for qualities of life of which others are reminded when they think of us. When you think of some people, you smile because they are funny. Their names suggest fun or laughter. Some people are so joyless that their names might stand for grumpy. There are persons who are so selfish that you have one thought suggested by their names, and that is that they are greedy. Others are so unselfish that we are reminded of kindness. On and on we could go in thinking about the names of people and what we think of whenever we hear their names.

The meanings of names in Bible times were attached to those names when they were given to those persons at birth. We have the power to create impressions, to make our names stand for something good or bad, to be remembered by others as nice or ugly persons.

Those choices begin very early. We need to think about the kind of persons we are and the kind of people we want to become. We must be willing to admit that some things inside of us need correction and to do what is necessary for those conditions to be changed. Parents can help us with that, but we can help ourselves as well. We must give people good things to think about when they think about us.

# What Does It Mean?

You may have noticed that a dog will turn his head a bit to one side at times when he hears a peculiar noise. It is though he were asking, "What is that? What does it mean?"

You may have heard a word used that you had not heard before and wondered, *What does it mean?* Some of you are old enough to use the dictionary. You can find the answer to your question by looking up that word. That is a good habit to form and to follow for the remainder of your life. Looking up words will help you know their meanings. Using them will help you express yourself.

Life has many experiences of joy and instruction that we recognize immediately. Even those, however, we will think about later, and new meanings will come to us. Music is like that. Great music lasts on and on. We listen to it over and over. It is like a spring that never runs dry. Every visit to it supplies a special need.

Great books are like that as well. Some passages and poems we can read and reread, and fresh meanings keep coming to us.

Life's everyday experiences, like sunshine, rain, breathing, seeing, hearing, conversation, and laughter, will mean most when we think enough to ask, at least occasionally, "What do they mean?"

There are events that puzzle us. They may involve difficulties and suffering. We will do well to ask of such a happening, "What does it mean?" God may be able to bring to light meanings of which we had not thought.

When something good happens to you, you may ask, "What does it mean?" And from that you may be even happier. When something sad happens to you, you may ask, "What does it mean?" And from that you may become a finer and more loving person.

# Why Not Free the Grass and Let the Lawn Grow?

Mowing a lawn is a lot of trouble and work. To get the mower cranked is the first thing. Then back and forth across the yard one must go, taking the lawn one strip at a time until the whole job is done. It takes a lot of patience and energy to mow the lawn.

Why do it anyway? Why go to the trouble? Why not let the grass grow wild and quit interfering with it? The answer is simple. Only a neatly mowed, well-trimmed lawn is pretty. Pass a lawn that is grown up and gone to seed, and you know that either the house is deserted or nobody cares. Everybody knows that a yard is not supposed to look like that.

There are some people who allow children to have their own way much of the time even though it means inconvenience to others and destruction of property. It reminds me of a lawn that is allowed to grow without any interference from anyone. Children who are allowed to grow up wild like the grass do not make a pretty sight. Parents may love a child who acts disrespectful and ugly, but nobody else will.

My mother used to say that it hurt her worse than it did me when she punished me for something that I had done. I always found that a little hard to believe! As I look back on it now, I am sure that she must have been right, and I am sure that the discipline that I got did me good. I am thankful that she did not let me grow wild like an untended lawn. She cared too much for that.

When we cannot have our way, it could be that our way is not a good way. Sometimes what we want to do is not what we should do.

When grass is turned loose, it looks awful. So does life!

# Following the Map

When your family goes on vacation, one of the things that you need before you get started is a road map. Some service stations give these away to their customers. They have highways of all sorts marked on them. Towns and cities are there. The number of miles from one place to another is written on the map. Interesting things to see along the way are found on maps as well.

Before our children got old enough to drive, they would find the place where we were going on the map. Then they would find where we were. As we would go from one town to another, they would trace our trip on the map and tell us what the next town would be. They would have a good time following the map.

You may want to get a map to see where you live, where the nearest beach is, where the mountains are, and other interesting facts. Studying a map can be fun.

In living, we need to know where we are going and how to get there. Without a map on a trip we would lose our way. Without knowing where we are going and the directions for getting there in our lives, we will wander around and get lost.

The Bible is a good map for us in living. It is not made up like a road map, but it serves the purpose of telling us where our destination is and something about the journey to it. There are some things about the Bible that none of us can understand. Those are not the things we are talking about here. There are many parts of the Bible that are clear and easy for a child to understand.

The place where we want to go is a life with God for God. There is nothing else like that. God made us, and he wants us to be with him. He tells us that life with him is the good and happy life.

As we learn to pray, worship in the church, and help others when they need us, we are on our way to this full, good life in God.

The Bible is a book — but it is a map, too, because we are able to find in it where we want to go and how to get there.

26

# "Look Where You Are Going!"

When somebody has bumped into you at home or at school, you may have said a little impatiently, "Look where you are going!" No doubt about it, people should be more careful. That goes for walking, riding a bike, or driving a car. The other day I found myself on the wrong road because at an intersection I had failed to see the sign pointing in the right direction. I did not look carefully enough, or I would have seen it.

Think about that in living. "Look where you are going" is good advice.

A person can lose the way by not looking where he or she is going. Carelessness does that. Interest in the wrong things is a sign that we have missed the right road. A person may miss the right road because he or she does not see it. The person does not see it because he or she is not looking for it. That is not where his or her interest lies.

From our earliest years we begin making choices. Our parents make many decisions for us, but we make some on our own. The older a child grows, the more decisions he or she will be called upon to make. We need to exercise care that we move in the right direction, that we look carefully where we are going.

When people get lost, it is possible to get back on the right track. Jesus teaches us that. It is called forgiveness. It means a change in the things you love and want. We all need that, because even the best person is far from perfect.

There are some things, however, that we are spared asking forgiveness for if we look where we are going and think and pray. It saves a lot of heartache for ourselves and disappointment for others when we take the right road in the beginning.

Let us spare ourselves and those whom we love as much hurt as possible through avoiding choices that do people harm.

Look where you are going! It always pays.

# Your Family Treasure

If your father should discover a treasure chest somewhere, left there by pirates or explorers, you would think that your family had come into a great treasure. You would call your friends and tell them of the excitement in your family and what it was all about. Families do have treasures in things that have not been accidentally discovered but left to them by other members of that family or by friends. Those treasures may include clocks, silver, china, antiques, rugs, and jewelry. People prize these things because others have loved them, and they have loved the people who loved them. Some treasures people have acquired for themselves. They value them because of their quaintness or beauty.

Every adult and child who loves his or her family should think, however, in terms not only of things of value that the eye can see, but also of treasures that are in the heart. Those can be exciting too!

Memory is one of those possessions. Good times have a way of lingering in the mind, and people recall scenes and faces and voices that were precious to them. Favorite family stories are told over and over, and we laugh at them as often as they are told, because they never get old. Special days and occasions, including Thanksgiving, Christmas, birthdays, and graduations, are thought of time and again years after they have happened. They are priceless treasures.

Family love is a form of wealth that is very important. People may not have much money, but if they love one another they are wealthy. If they have trust and respect and appreciation in their hearts for one another, they are rich!

Family treasure is more than money. It is things that money can't buy. Nobody can steal this sort of treasure. It is secure as long as people live. You are part of your family's wealth. You love and are loved. There is no way to beat that for true riches!

# A Smile Is like the Sun

Sunshine is one of the great blessings that we enjoy. While we sleep, there is darkness. When we wake up in the morning, the earth is often bathed in glorious sunlight. In its light we can see the blue sky, the white clouds, the fresh green of trees in spring, the lush green in summer, and the beautiful colors of the leaves in the fall. Flowers seem to lift up their heads in the morning, cheered by the morning sun. The leaves of some plants will follow the sun from east to west as the day goes on. Sunlight brings fresh energy and new life to nature and to people.

A smile is like the sun. There is a lot of difference between a frown and a smile on the same face. It requires many more muscles to frown, I am told, than it does to smile. A frown is not pleasant to look at. It makes us want to look somewhere else. The person who frowns is not very happy at the time, and he or she makes other people uncomfortable as well.

The same face that frowns is capable of a smile. A smile is something that everybody understands. It does not have to be explained. It is a sign of joy. It brings cheer like the morning sunshine.

There is something sad about an adult and about a child who find it difficult to smile. God made us with the power to be pleasant, to look pleasant, and to show goodwill and friendship with a smile.

My day is always brighter when I am spoken to by a child and when there is a smile behind that greeting. It makes me glad that we saw each other. After that I go on my way thinking, *What a nice, bright child!*

A pleasant face makes home a happy place. It brightens a schoolroom. It makes church a friendly place to be. It helps a neighborhood be a good one.

Children loved Jesus. They were not afraid of him. They came to him readily. It must have been because he had a loving face and one that knew how to smile in a warm, friendly way.

The friends of Jesus, people whom we call Christians, are loving and friendly and joyful as he was. He wants us to be that way. There are some things that we cannot do. But there is one thing that we all can do — smile!

# A Plastic Jug, a Beer Can, and a Mountain Stream

Our family went on a beautiful ride one summer afternoon. We left the main highway and went down a mountainside to the bottom of a valley. It is the loveliest place that anybody would want to see. There were houses with rock chimneys that made us think about winter and how in the coldest weather, with snow everywhere, blue smoke would be curling out of them and warm fires would be keeping the people snug inside. Some of those houses had colorful beds of flowers growing around them that told us that somebody who lived there loved beauty and loved home.

Near one of those places was a bridge across a rushing stream. We drove across it and got out to look at it. Tumbling down the hill from another direction was another stream that joined the other one right where the bridge crossed. I was ready to enjoy the unspoiled beauty of that scene when I looked down at the point where the streams came together and there was a plastic jug caught in some rocks and a beer can on the bottom of the stream. I tried not to look at them, to see the beautiful things that were there in spite of them, and to listen to the music of the water as it came tumbling down.

It was hard to do that. I kept thinking about the people who did not give beauty a thought and who did not care what they messed up for other people. How poor in heart they were!

God has created a beautiful world. There is no admission charge. The world is like a garden that belongs to God, and he has selected us to enjoy it and to help him keep it. With so many people in the world, if we are careless, we can abuse it and destroy it. Where that happens, it is very sad.

It is wrong to make something beautiful into something ugly. There are so many lovely sights to see, beautiful places to visit. God allows us the privilege of seeing some of them. All he asks is that we help him care for them so that others may enjoy them too. That is a part of his will for our lives.

# A Shepherd and His Sheep

A shepherd is one who cares for sheep. He or she looks out for them at all times. When they are out in the field the shepherd is there to protect them. In some parts of the world there are wild animals that kill sheep if they can get to them. The shepherd protects them from the wild animals. The shepherd guides the sheep to places where there is grass to eat and water to drink.

In the evening this one who is in charge of the sheep brings them to a place where they rest and sleep. Such a place is called the sheepfold. The shepherd sleeps with them and sees to it that no harm comes to them.

Jesus told a story about a shepherd and a herd of sheep. He said that a shepherd had one hundred sheep. All day long they were out in the field. One sheep somehow wandered off from the rest. The shepherd failed to see what happened. Perhaps it got behind a rock and then out of sight of the good shepherd and nibbled its way farther and farther from the others.

That night when they got to the sheepfold, the shepherd counted the animals. One, two, three, four, and so on, until he got to ninety-nine. That was all. He counted again. There were only ninety-nine. One was missing. He was troubled over it. What would he do?

He hardly had to think about it. He left the ninety-nine that were safe in the fold and went out into the night looking for the missing sheep. He probably had a good idea where he might find the lost one. He knew the sheep so well that he knew which one was missing. He could not bear the thought of that helpless animal out there in some lonely place wondering where everybody was, wishing it were with the others and wishing for its good master. So off he went. He searched until he found it and brought it back to the fold.

Jesus said that people are like sheep and that he is the shepherd. He loves his sheep very much. He cannot bear the thought of a sheep's wandering away and being destroyed. So he goes and looks until he finds it. He loves every person that much. Every person is important, and he wants us to be with him always. It helps us live with contented hearts to know that he loves us that much. What would we do without him!?

# "Please Open the Door!"

Coming into the house with your toys in your hands, you may have called to someone inside, "Please open the door."

Look at that request and see what it says. It says that we need other people. There come times when we are not able to do for ourselves what needs to be done, and other people help. Those times, in fact, come every day. As dependent as we are on other people, we need to be thoughtful and grateful to them for what they do for us. It is a world in which we travel with others or we do not travel at all.

Turn it around and look at it this way. Perhaps you have been in the house and have heard someone call, "Please open the door." It may have been your mother with groceries or your father with packages or your brother or sister trying to get in with arms full of something. Somebody else is not the door opener. You are! It is your chance to help.

Think about the doors themselves. Doors are good for keeping things out. They keep out cold air in the winter and hot air in the summer. They keep out stray dogs and cats. They keep out people who have no business in your house.

A house must have doors. How else would we get in and out, and how would other people whom we love to see come to visit us? We must be selective about what comes through the doors of our house. We decide what comes in and what stays out.

That is true of life. Life has its doors. They are to keep some things out. Bad thoughts, ugly, hurtful words, selfish acts are to be kept out. It is a good thing to have doors of the mind to keep them out.

There are good uses for those doors, however, as the best thoughts and habits are allowed to come through them.

So — I guess we should always ask when a knock comes on the door, "Who is it?" And when a knock comes to the door of the mind, we should ask, "Who is it, and what do you want?"

# Life in an Anthill

Ants are interesting little creatures. Ants can be ugly when they want to be, as anybody knows who has ever walked across an anthill barefoot or stood too close to one without knowing that the ants were close. They figure, I guess, that people are their enemies and that they must defend themselves. They are tiny, but they can let you know right away that they are there.

In spite of that, there are some good things that people can learn from ants and in what we learn from them they can be our friends.

If you do your jobs willingly and well around the house, someone may say that you are smart. Ants are smart. They are not afraid of work. They set themselves to digging their tunnels in the ground. These tunnels are their homes. One particle at a time, they haul enough soil out of the ground to make their underground home.

We learn from the ant that work is important. This country that we love got its start with people who were not afraid of work. The church is what it is largely because of good people who have worked in it. A home is a secure and happy fellowship of people who work at making it what it is. The father and perhaps the mother work to make enough money to pay the bills. Parents and children work within it to make it a home of which they can be proud. You have already learned that it takes work to do well in school. Not many students who are lazy make good grades. A good student pays attention at school and makes it a practice of doing the homework.

Another lesson we learn from the anthill is that of cooperation, or working together. One ant could never provide that safe underground home alone. They help one another in doing the digging. Then, too, they work together in storing their food. If you have noticed them at work, you may have seen them carrying small particles of food into that little hole in the ground to use when they need it.

Here again it takes cooperation, people working together, to make a great country, to have an effective church, and to create and keep a good home. The little ant teaches us things that stay with us and that do us good.

# Your Face Speaks

We can understand what people are thinking and how they feel by their words. Words are powerful to express what people think and what they feel toward other persons and about issues. Words speak sharply or lovingly what we want other persons to know.

Words are not the only means that we have of telling our thoughts and attitudes. Facial expressions at times can show this even better than words. Your face speaks.

A face can display anger. A look at an angry person's eyes will tell the tale.

A face can reveal one's embarrassment. Sometimes it will turn red, and one will look down or aside as though to try to escape.

Sometimes a face will say that a person does not understand. You may look like that at school when the teacher says something that you do not understand.

Sorrow is shown on a face. Let grief come, and the lines of one's face speak their message of loss. Disappointed, sorrowful eyes are one of the saddest things in the world.

A face can speak joy. When a person is happy, the face shows it. We can speak words to cheer other people, and this at times is good. A cheerful face can do far more, however, than cheerful words. More people see your face than hear you speak. A bright, smiling, happy face is one of the great treasures of the world.

A bright face shows that one is happy, and it helps to keep one happy. Your face has a connection with your life within. The friends of Jesus may have their moments when they are downcast or discouraged, but when he lives in their hearts, they have a way of recovering from those conditions and moods. A person who loves Jesus has peace. Jesus lives on the inside, and it shows on the outside.

Watch what happens to your heart, because people are always watching your face. Take care of your heart, and your face will take care of itself.

# A Deaf Old Lady with a Bouquet of Flowers

My childhood was spent in a town much smaller than most of you know anything about. The church in which I was reared was a little one. They did things in a way that might seem odd to you.

For example, we all met in the sanctuary, where the preaching services were held, for Sunday school. We would sing and have a prayer, and then the superintendent of the Sunday school would tell us to go to our classes. After we had been there awhile, he would use a little tap bell to let us know that it was time to come back together. The church was so small that the bell could be heard easily wherever the classes were meeting. One tap on the bell meant that the time was almost up and that the teachers were to finish. Two taps on the bell meant that Sunday school was over and that the classes were to come back together. That might seem strange to you.

In that community there was a very old lady, a member of that church, who was completely deaf. She couldn't even hear thunder. The fact that she was deaf did not keep her from coming to church. She was there every Sunday. She had her favorite place to sit. She sat there during the service, and the only way she knew when the service was over was when the other people got up. She did not know what was being said, but she knew where she was. She knew that she was in God's house with God's people. She was happy, and in her own way she worshiped in her heart in that place with her friends.

This dear old deaf lady would bring a little bouquet of flowers for the church every Sunday morning. It did not matter to her if another larger arrangement was already there. She would bring hers and place it there as well. I can see her in my mind now many a hot Sunday morning coming up the hill with a handful of flowers for that church. It was something that she could do, and she did it. She loved God, and she loved the church. She offered her flowers, and she offered herself. I believe God must have said to her, "Thank you. You have done well."

# Training Your Eyes

One day our daughter, Martha, and I were on a trip out of town We were passing through a little town that is not known for it: beauty. As we pulled off from the traffic light, I said to her, "Look at that ugly building on the corner."

Almost in the same breath, she exclaimed, "Look at the beautiful flowers in that yard."

I felt ashamed. I saw the ugly. She saw the beautiful.

We see largely what we train our eyes to see. We often find what our eyes are trained to look for.

Seeing the bad and looking for the beautiful represent two approaches to life. Eyesight is not the only thing that picks up on that. We can expect to find the bad in people and find it. There is plenty wrong with people — including ourselves. It is possible to be so critical of other persons that we don't see anything but what ought not to be there. Many people are too hard on themselves. They have a low opinion of themselves. That is an unfortunate habit for the mind to form.

There is another direction in which to look, however, and that is toward the discovery of something good in people. This includes ourselves. There is something worthwhile, something good, in everybody. There would be a lot more good in people who seem almost all bad if they were encouraged in a kind way.

We can think about home in either of these two ways. We look for the bad, or we find the good.

That division of thought comes in the church. All some people can do is criticize the church. Others look for the good — and find it.

The critical people are not very happy with others or with themselves. The gentle, loving people are the happy ones. They see the good and try to create good wherever they are.

# The Treasure of Pictures

A camera is a fine piece of equipment. Go anywhere on vacation or sight-seeing, and you will find people with cameras hanging around their necks. What is happening to them is important. They want to remember those scenes. They take pictures to help them remember.

At weddings the photographer is almost as important as the bride. After the wedding service pictures are taken of the bride and groom, of the wedding party, of family groups. Every November twelfth my wife and I get out our wedding pictures. We think again about our happy wedding. We think about how much the others in the picture have changed since then and how little we have!

School pictures are important to you. There is usually conversation at the breakfast table on the morning that school pictures are to be taken. Your mothers have probably helped you select what you are to wear that day. Fathers and mothers carry pictures of you in their billfolds and pocketbooks. Some of your pictures you give to your friends.

Your mind is a kind of picture album. In it are stored many scenes that you have visited. You remember how people look. You can see clearly in your mind how things were. It has been a long time since my childhood, but I can remember so well how my teachers looked. I can remember some places that my family and I visited that impressed me. I am always thankful for the picture book of the mind that we call memory.

Usually we can remember better when we try to remember. It would be well if you could make it a practice of remembering the beautiful things, the meaningful things. These pictures in your mind will be a great treasure as you grow older. They can bring brightness and gladness. Many times if you remember something good it can help you make the right decision when you need to make it.

# A Violet by
# a Mountain Path

Many people work hard to provide for their families. Fathers and mothers put in long hours at their jobs and in keeping a house and yard clean and attractive. It is good for them to have some time away from it occasionally. Let me tell you about what happened to our family on one of those relaxing days.

We went on an outing to one of the most beautiful places that you could find anywhere. We crossed a mountain stream that came tumbling down from the mountain and started up a peaceful path through the woods.

We walked very slowly because there were so many interesting things to see. Trees and shrubs and ferns were all along to draw our attention. Suddenly one of our party stopped and picked the loveliest, most delicate violet. We looked at its color and form, and all of us exclaimed about how beautiful it was.

That violet was one of the tiniest flowers that I have ever seen. There in all of that mountain vastness was that little violet occupying its own special place. I would probably have passed that little flower without seeing it, but that family member had an eye for it, and he found it.

We live in a world in which many people think that bigness is about the only thing that counts. If we believe Jesus at all, that is far from right. One day he and a large crowd of people were far from a place where they could get food at mealtime. One disciple said that a child was there with some barley loaves and fish, but he did not think that this was enough to do any good. Jesus used what that child had and performed a miracle, and all the people were fed. We don't know how that happened, but that boy with his small lunch was the beginning of it all.

We need to be careful not to be thrown off by bigness. There are many little things that are important. Some very beautiful things are very tiny things, and God has given them their own special places. Perhaps we should ask God to give us eyes to see everything that he has made, "all things bright and beautiful; all creatures great and small," and be thankful.

# A Runaway for a Day

When I was a small boy, I would become angry at times with my mother. One day when that happened, I jumped on my bicycle without telling her good-bye and rode a mile out into the country to the home of my aunt and uncle. They had a son who was about my age. We played together many a happy day in our childhood. We walked in the fields, tramped through the woods, played in the big yard, ate scuppernongs in season, and went swimming in hot weather in the swimming hole.

It was to that country home and to the company of my cousin that my anger took me that day.

It was hot, and we headed for our swimming hole as fast as our legs would carry us. We dived and swam until that became too tame. Then we decided to do some tricks at diving. On one of those tricks I did a flip over the shoulders of my cousin in shallow water. It took me straight down, and my head hit the bottom with a wham! I came up with a cut on the top of my head. I carry the scar of that accident until this day. My neck could have been broken and I could have died on the spot, or I could have been paralyzed for life. Fortunately neither of those things happened.

Coming up out of the water, I had had enough swimming for that day. I wanted to go home. Do you know whom I wanted to see? My mother! I forgot about my anger of that morning. Whatever she had done to me did not seem so bad after all.

I got on my bicycle and pedaled myself home. She hadn't worried about me too much because she knew where I was and that I would be home when the sun began to go down.

My mother didn't say, "It serves you right, getting angry with me and running away." She was distressed about my head and about what I could have done to myself in that accident. She gave me some first-aid treatment and comforted me.

I think God must be like that when we run away from him. He wants us back, loves us before we come back and when we do come back. My mother was a loving mother who forgave me. God is a loving Father who forgives us. It is good that he is like that. "We love him because he first loved us" and because he keeps on loving us always.

# Some Shapes of Your Hands

The hand is one of the most useful parts of the human body. Occasionally you see a person who has no hands. They may have been lost in war or in an accident. We who have two good hands wonder how a person manages who has none. Hands are not only useful in getting things done, but they can also express our feelings just as a facial expression can tell other persons what we are thinking.

Think of the hand when it is shaped as a fist. It shows that a person is disturbed or angry. When I was a boy, I would get into fights occasionally. It was not a good thing, I am sure, but it happened. The only weapon that I can ever remember using was fists.

Hands can show that one is upset and anxious. When there is deep trouble, one may wring his or her hands. As hands pull at each other, they seem to say that distress is pulling at one's heart.

Hands can be a picture of a heart that is greedy. The palms are turned up with fingers spread wide to get all there is to be had. Such a position of the hands stands for greedy desire. "Let me get all there is," those grasping hands seem to say.

Hands can be shaped for a handshake. For many years a handshake has been a friendly greeting. When one person meets another person and each gives the other the right hand, they may say words of greeting, but in the act of shaking hands they say something in addition to what they speak. Many hands are shaken at the church every Sunday, on the street when people meet, at clubs where members gather, in homes when hosts greet guests. It is a good custom.

Hands can be fixed in the position of prayer. You may have seen pictures of children saying their prayers. They are kneeling with hands together in front of them. It is a way that the body expresses the devotion of body and heart to God.

So, hands are not only good for work; they are also good for saying things. They say things about friendship, and they may help us pray. We need to avoid the ugly shapes of our hands and to think about how well we can use our hands in letting other people know the best and deepest feelings of our hearts.

# Wind

Wind is something we hear and feel but cannot see. We hear it whistling around the corner of the house on a cold night. If we were outside, we would shiver and wish for a warm, lighted house.

Wind can parch one's lips and blister one's face. Wind can make you hurt.

Wind can be very strong. In a hurricane or a tornado it can destroy property and take lives. On the seacoast, wind can lash the water against the shore and over sea walls, breaking them down and attacking houses and stores nearby.

In spite of the fact that wind can howl and make you lonely, make you cold on a winter night, blister your skin in summer, destroy property in a storm, wind is a very good thing.

Have you ever walked through the woods on a pleasant, sunny day and heard the wind sighing in the pines? It makes one feel relaxed and glad to be there.

A breeze is wonderful on a hot day. Before people had air conditioning, they sat on porches in the summertime to catch any breeze that might be stirring. Some people still prefer to sit outside, if it isn't too hot, to enjoy the fresh air.

The rainfall that is so necessary to life wouldn't be possible if it were not for currents of air blowing the clouds about and creating the conditions under which rain comes from them. The wind blows up a dark cloud, and we scurry for cover. From inside we look at the rain, and we know that plants, flowers, and people could not live without it.

Before the time of steamships the ships on the sea were driven with sails. Seamen knew how to put up those mighty sails in order to catch the wind and thus be carried where they wished to go. We in this country owe a great debt to the wind. The people who were not happy in Europe and who wanted to come here would never have made it without wind for the sails of their ships to bring them.

God gave us a good thing when he gave us the wind.

# Words

Have you ever seen a person who was deaf and dumb? I mean a person who cannot talk, who lives in a world without words. There is a sign language that such persons use with their hands that helps them in communicating with one another, but they live without speaking and hearing words. Aren't we blessed to be able to talk and to hear!

Language is an interesting study. Countries of the world have their own languages. Europe has so many visitors from all parts of the world that it is not unusual to meet a person who can speak three or four languages.

It is exciting when a baby is learning to talk. Parents say words over and over until the baby learns to say some very simple ones at first and as time goes on more and more words.

Words are powerful. They can cut and bruise. Words hot with anger can bring people to tears. Words can bring laughter. Words can paint pictures for the mind. Words can make us think. Words help us learn. Words make friendship and family life enjoyable through conversation.

English is a very beautiful language when it is spoken well. Think about some words that we know with meanings that we hold dear.

Love leads the list. Loves makes life worth living. To have your mother and father tell you that they love you makes you feel warm and good inside. To tell them that you love them expresses your sweet, tender feelings toward them.

Joy is another wonderful word. Peace is another one. Hope is another one. Trust is another one.

You might think about words that stand for things that mean the most to you. Thank God for words that we can speak and for words that we can hear. They help make life good when we use them well.

# Learning to Count

Our two-and-a-half-year-old twin grandsons are learning to count. Slowly, with a finger going up each time, they begin: one... two... three. And that's as far as they've gotten! Given time, though, they will learn to count just as high as you can.

Thinking about their learning to do that, my mind began to drift to the things that people do with their ability to count. One of the things that almost everybody likes to count is money. You may have already done something for the family or for a neighbor in return for which you received some money. You had reason to be proud of what you earned.

Fun as it can be at times, there is a danger in counting money. People come to love it too well, liking to keep it and count it. Money can take away more than it gives. It can rob a home of happiness if it is not used properly. It can drive a wedge between friends. It can cause a person to forget God. Important as money is when it is made honestly and used wisely, it can be an enemy of all higher values when it becomes the first thing and the main thing in a person's life. I hope these little twins will, as the years come and go, watch what kind of counting they do with money.

Bad things of one kind or another happen to everybody who lives very long. It is possible to count the bad times and forget the good ones. An emphasis on misfortune, on the things and the people that have caused one suffering, can form the headlines of the heart. Almost all some people think about is the unlucky turn that their lives have taken, the bad news that has found its way to their doors. Such thoughts as those are not healthy.

To count your blessings is a far better thing to do. I hope our little twins will learn to do that early in their lives. There is so much good that happens. It would be interesting to try to count those times and count the ways.

# Like a Tree

When you look at a tree, you see only part of that tree. Some of it is above ground. A large part of it is below the ground. It takes it all to make the tree.

The parts that we see are the trunk, the limbs, the leaves. If it is a fruit tree, we see the fruit. A beautiful tree is one of the loveliest things that can be found anywhere.

Below the ground is the root structure. Most trees have a tap root. It goes straight down into the ground and helps hold the top part up when the wind blows against it. Roots go in all directions to take in water and food from the soil. Some of the roots are large, and others are very small. Without that root system the tree would die and topple over.

In the middle of the Bible is a book called the Psalms. It is a collection of hymns, many of which are very beautiful. In the first Psalm there is the description of a good man. He resembles a tree that draws its freshness and strength from a nearby stream and that can be depended upon to bear its fruit.

A fine person is like a fruit tree. You can't see the inner life of a person. It is like the roots of the tree. Without those, the tree can't live. Without that inner life in a person there is nothing to him or her. As the roots bring water and food into the tree, so prayer and Bible reading bring spiritual water and food into the life of a person. A person may be helped by thinking good thoughts and by reading about what it means to be a Christian.

The church is like the air and energy from the sun to the leaves of the plant. The plant could not live without those things that it gets from the air and from the sun.

That fruit tree takes in and takes in until the beautiful fruit appears. That's the way good people are. They take into their lives what prayer, Bible reading, and good thoughts can give. They also receive what the church has to share. They break out like good fruit in lives that are sound and strong.

You are little trees. We must be careful that you do not grow crooked, but straight and beautifully, and that you have everything to grow on that a little tree ought to have.

# Watch What You Throw in the Trash Can

Trash cans are handy things to have around the house. Bathrooms, bedrooms, family rooms have trash cans, not to mention the garbage can in the kitchen. Many times a day it becomes necessary to find the nearest trash can to put something into it. The house would soon be knee-deep in paper and litter if those cans were not there. They are in convenient places for our use in placing things in them that are worn out or no longer have a purpose.

Garbage trucks come by often to empty the big cans that we have been filling day after day. Tons and tons of garbage and trash are hauled away every week.

I wonder how much of that is necessary. If we knew that we could not get a replacement for some article, would we be as likely to throw away the one we have?

When I have misplaced a sheet of paper or a letter, I have looked through the trash can to see whether I had thrown it away without meaning to do so. It could have been carelessly tossed away when I meant to keep it. It occurs to me that I could have also been that careless about something that I intended to throw away but that I should have kept for further use.

In a time of high prices and shortages, I have found myself tearing off and saving the bottom half of a sheet of paper on which I had made a mistake. I have seen the time when I would have wadded up the whole thing and tossed it into the trash can.

You may have thrown toys away that some child would have been happy to have.

We live in a throwaway time, when so much that is manufactured is to be used only once and discarded. If that becomes habit with us, casting aside things that are designed to be more permanent, we will pay a heavy penalty in years to come.

No matter how much money we may have, to be throwaway people is wrong.

# The Parable of the Water Tank

The sight of a water tank usually means that a town is near. As it comes into view when we are traveling along a highway, we know that people are there. Homes, fire departments, factories, schools need water. The water tank is there to be sure that they get it.

There are two processes that go on in a water tank. The tank receives water, and it gives out water.

Somewhere there is a well sunk deep into the earth. A pump is set up to bring the water to the surface and then into the tank. The tank wouldn't be any good without the well. The tank receives the water from the well through a pipe. There are pipes, in turn, that lead from the tank to all parts of the town. Thus the tank takes in water and gives out water, and the people's needs are met.

Life is like one of those tanks. We receive gifts from God. He provides all that we have. Like the well that gives water to thirsty people, God gives us all the good things that we have. We do not create these good things. God gives them, and we take them, as that tank takes in water.

The action doesn't stop with our receiving the blessings of God, just as the tank does not take in water without giving it out. We are blessed by receiving, and others are blessed by our giving. It is also true the other way: we are blessed by our giving, and others are blessed by receiving.

The process of good fortune is never to stop with us. When that happens, selfishness is at work. If the tank held the water and never gave it out, the water would lose its freshness. It would become stale and unfit to drink.

Happy, rewarding living takes place when the flow of joys is to us and through us. Life is not "give and take"; it is take and give.

# Clean Your Plate

When I was a child and took more on my plate than I could eat, my mother would say, "Your eyes were bigger than your stomach." She frowned on this, and she should have.

To heap one's plate with food that is more than enough to satisfy the appetite makes one greedy. It isn't very thoughtful because in doing that we may have taken someone else's share.

To take more than one needs is to take what somebody else needs who may not be at the table. It could be a child in a faraway place who does not have enough to eat.

More than half the people on earth go to bed hungry every night. Many people starve to death every day.

Some countries that have fewer people and are more advanced than others are trying to help the developing countries grow more food for their people. It is not easy. They do not have training and equipment that are adequate.

The number of people in the world continues to grow. Sincere, concerned Christian people in many places are trying to help solve the aching problem of hunger.

The Bible tells us that Jesus fed hungry people. It hurt him to see them hungry. He could not enjoy food himself when so many others did not have enough.

Perhaps you could help do that in your own way. One way you can help is not to waste, not to take more food than you can eat or need, to clean your plate.

When we do that we will be more thankful to God for what we do have. We may be reminded to pray for people who suffer. We may also be prompted to do other things to help them in their need.

# Books

Some people think that books are for students much older than you or for grown-ups. All one has to do to see that such is not the case is to visit a bookstore or the book section of a department store. There are shelves and tables filled with books for children just your age. On Christmas morning many a child wakes up to find that some colorful and interesting books are a part of Christmas, along with toys and clothes.

Long before a child can talk, he or she becomes interested in books. Children can learn objects and when asked where something is on a page point to it instantly. There are books that help a child learn to count, learn about animals, things in the natural world, food, furniture, and other items in a household.

Books for children a little older than those who are just beginning to sit still to be read to are made up of stories. Children come to love those and want them read and reread. They come to know them by heart, so that if one word is read wrong they will know it and correct the reader.

Books are interesting. The older you grow, the more you will read and the more you will learn. If you develop a love for books, you will not associate them with a world of study that you wish you could get away from. Books become our friends. I can go into my study at home at night and in the dark almost put my hands on the books that I want. They are there as my faithful friends waiting to help me in my work.

As you grow older, you will gather books of your own. Books open to us interesting things about people — what they have thought and done and places where they have gone. Books bring to our eyes and minds the great art of the world. Books can be entertaining as well as educational.

Someday one of you may write a book. Who knows? But there is one thing for sure, all of us can read books. That is something for which to be thankful.

# Turn on the Light

Sometimes when a family comes into a dark house, a person other than the first one in will say, "Turn on the light." Somebody hits the light switch, and the room is flooded with light.

A dark house is not inviting. An old, large, dark house that sits back from the street surrounded by low-hanging trees even looks spooky. To try to find one's way around in a dark room may cause one to walk into something.

Light in a house looks like life. It appears that people are at home and the place is not deserted.

It would be a dark world without good people in it. Jesus once told some people whom he was depending on that they were lights in the world. Jesus also referred to himself as light and said that those who stayed close to him would not be in darkness. We light up when his light comes into our lives. Darkness is driven out. Cheerful, radiant light is everywhere.

Sometimes churches have services of lights at Christmastime. Everyone is given a candle. A candle is burning on the altar. All other lights in the church are out. Someone will light a candle from the one on the altar. That person will light the candle of the next person, and that one will light the candle of the next person, and so on until the light in the church becomes brighter and brighter as candle after candle is lighted. Finally every person is holding a burning candle. The church would be a little darker if any candle were not burning.

Jesus says that the light that shines in every life is important. The cheer, the kindness, the encouragement that every person gives to others shine like lights. This world needs all the light that it can get.

Your life can bring joy that will be like turning on a light in somebody's heart. You can make that happen.

# Take Good Care of Your Friends

After two people have been together for a time and they start to part, one of them may say to the other, "Take good care of yourself!"

The other will reply, "You do the same."

There are some things that one ought to do in taking care of oneself, such as keeping the rules of good health and trying to stay out of trouble. Another fine thing to do is to take good care of your friends. Every friendship should bear the label HANDLE WITH CARE! Friendship is a precious possession, and it can easily slip away if people do not take good care of it.

What are some things that you can do in taking care of your friends? For one thing, you speak nicely to them. People do not enjoy being spoken to in an ugly or thoughtless way. An apology may be given and accepted, but it is better to have left the harsh word unsaid. Consideration in the words and the tone that one uses in speaking to people is important in keeping friendship strong.

Another way to preserve friendship is to listen to your friends when they have something to say to you. Some people are not very good listeners. They get a faraway look in their eyes that shows that they are not paying attention. What another person says is important. Learn to listen.

Doing nice things for your friends is another way of drawing even closer to them. Some people think about what other persons can give to them and do for them. A better thing is to think and to plan ways to let our friends know just how much we think of them and how glad we are that the friendship does exist.

Early in your life, if you make it a habit of being a friend to others, you will never be without friends. They and you will be the better for it.

# Helping to Make Others Happy

The world is crowded with miserable people. Many of them are made unhappy by the actions of other people. Maybe those whom they have trusted have let them down. The harsh words and unkind treatment that are handed out by evil or even careless persons can cause deep hurt.

There are other people who make themselves miserable. They are too selfish to be happy. Life for them has self at the center. A self-centered person can never be truly happy. Life is not geared up that way. Happiness is not something that a person finds by seeking it and making it the most important thing in life. Happiness does not come that way.

The real way to live is to make others happy. One will be happy in doing this but will not do so just to get rewards. It will be done because of the joy that it brings to others.

Jesus was always trying to bring cheer to downcast people. He wanted them to have joy. He served other persons and made them his friends. He said that the greatest people in the world are those who do things for others. They do not try to get things done for themselves. They try to do helpful things for other persons, to lift burdens, to be friendly, loving, and caring.

I wonder if you are beginning to know the joy of that kind of living. To think about other people is the starting point. To get one's mind off oneself and begin thinking about the needs of others is the point that we need to master in our minds. This can be done at home, with one's friends, among the people of the neighborhood.

Forget self. Remember others. That is the way to live.

# Pick Up Your Clothes

"Don't forget to pick up your clothes!" Even the youngest of you have probably heard your mothers say that. You will probably hear it again.

The older you grow, the more things you will be able to do for yourselves. Picking up your clothes, books, and toys is something that you can do now.

Parents have a steady job in looking after you and in doing all the necessary and loving things that have to be done in the homes where you live. There are groceries to buy, meals to prepare, dishes to clean, the laundry to do. Add to those cleaning the house, taking children places, going to meetings, and too many other things to mention. Every child should ask, "What can I do to help?"

There are many ways to help. You may have already found that it is fun to feel a part of your home by helping where you can. To do helpful things like picking up your clothes without being told is the very best thing you can do.

Forming habits like that reduces your dependence on other people and keeps them from having to do things for you that you can do for yourselves. One of the things this will do for you in later life is to make it unnecessary for other people to come along after you to clean up your mess. Many grown people have not learned that art.

Consideration of others is important. Every person has about all he or she can do. Dumping our unfinished tasks on others is bad.

So, get started young. Be as helpful and as independent as you can. You will like yourself better, and others will have reason to think more of you.

# The Steering Wheel

When you become fifteen years old, you will probably go to the state patrol office to get your learner's license to drive a car. On your sixteenth birthday you will be able to receive your full license and drive an automobile by yourself.

Long before I was old enough to drive, I would get behind the steering wheel of our family car when the motor was not running, turn it back and forth, make noises like a car makes when it is in motion, and play that I was driving the car. It was great fun, and I enjoyed entertaining myself that way many, many times.

I knew then what a steering wheel would do. You know what it will do from watching your parents or your brothers or sisters who are old enough to drive. The steering wheel is one of the most important parts of a car. Even if everything else is in top shape, a car cannot go without a steering wheel. A steering wheel gives guidance to the car and safety to the people in it. It helps the driver stay out of danger areas. It helps the people in the car arrive safely where they wish to go.

Our consciences are like steering wheels. The conscience helps us tell right from wrong. It cheers us when we choose right. It makes us feel bad when we do wrong. That steering wheel of the conscience helps us stay out of danger areas with our lives just as a car's steering wheel helps a driver do that. The steering wheel of the conscience helps keep us from having wrecks with our lives. It helps us get through a day as we should and make good choices. The thoughts we think, the words we say, the things we do happen because of what we do with that steering wheel in our minds called the conscience.

You are already behind that steering wheel, so use it well.

# What Do You See in the Mirror?

When you look into the mirror, what do you see? Yourself, of course. What is yourself? You see your hair. You see your nose, and you may wonder how it got to be like that! You see your eyes and think that they are pretty. You look at your teeth. You may look at your cheeks and think that you are getting fat. You smile into the mirror, and you might think that it is sad that you do not smile more often, as nice as that smile is. You see all of these parts and movements of your face and head. But are they you?

What is behind those eyes? What kind of person lives in that brain that is behind that face that you see in the mirror? Do you see a harsh or a kind person in that mirror? Every day we make choices to be one or the other. It is possible to lose patience with other people, to blame them for things that they did but could not help, to raise your voice and say hurtful words in hurtful ways.

If you choose to be so, you may look at a kind person in the mirror, someone whose temper is under control, who remembers that you might have made the same mistake that someone else made. You may be a person with tender feelings toward older people, helping get things for them or answering their questions. You can be helpful to your parents and to your brothers and sisters.

When you look into the mirror, you look at more than a face. You look at a thinking and acting person. On that basis, each person decides what he or she sees.

# Happy People Sing

Christmas is a time when people like to sing. The carols that we sing in church are beautiful. We sing them year after year, but they never grow old.

At Christmas, churches often have special musical programs. Choirs and soloists rehearse for weeks in preparation for such a time of worship.

Families sometimes gather around the piano at home and sing the carols and other popular Christmas songs as well.

It is the good news that Jesus came into the world that makes us want to sing. We are happy because he brought so much love in his heart and had so much to tell us that brings us joy.

Many mornings I hear the little children singing, "Jesus loves me, this I know." It always does me good to hear it. I know that many other good things may be taught the children, but if that is being taught and believed by them we are on a safe course. We teach them to sing that because it is news to sing about.

Great hymns that we sing on Sunday mornings in our services of worship express thanksgiving and hope. Something happens to us inside when we sing together. We are singing that we believe something worth believing. We are trusting in God. We believe in his care.

Maybe when you are alone, you sing a song that you know, or whistle a tune. Usually you are happy when you do that. You are not angry at anybody. You are glad to be alive and to enjoy so many good things.

When you sing, you make others happy as well. That is one of our reasons for living, to try to bring sunshine and contentment to the lives of other people. They need us more than we think they do. We need them, of course, but they need us too. We can wear a sour face and cause others to dread meeting us, or we can be happy and carry a song in our hearts. Let's agree to do the second.

# The Honest Man Who Came Back

One afternoon my wife was in the checkout line in a neighborhood grocery store. Just as she approached the cash register, a man who had been in front of her came back with some money in his hand. "You gave me too much change," he said to the cashier.

The man handed the cashier the change, she thanked him, and he left.

My wife came home and told the family about what an impressive sight it was to see somebody so honest. It was the cashier's mistake. The man could have kept the money. Despite the fact that probably nobody would have found out that he had it, he came back with the money. He never even put it in his pocket. He did not have any struggle about what to do. He was an honest man.

How many people do you think would have done that? It is one thing to be honest when people are looking and when there is a chance of getting caught if you are not honest. It is another thing to be honest when nobody is looking and you could get away with keeping what is not yours if you chose to do so. The honest person is pressed from within to do right.

The Bible tells us that we are not to steal. That man did not put his hand in that cash drawer and take out any money, but he would have felt like a thief if he had kept what was mistakenly given him.

It is not fair to take from others what rightfully belongs to them. That is the reason the Bible speaks as it does about stealing.

You can take pride in and enjoy what is yours. To be able to possess it and use it if you made it or earned it or received it as a gift is right and good. But it is better to have an empty hand than to have money in it that doesn't belong there.

# Boundaries of the Parking Space

A boundary is the edge of something. The boundary of a country is the place where that country ends. A land boundary is as far as a farmer can plow without getting on somebody else's property.

A parking space has boundaries. Many times you have been with some older person in your family to a shopping center, downtown, or at church. There are lines that mark where one is to park. You may have noted that the car is over one of the lines and said so to whoever was driving. With that the door was unlocked, the motor started, and another effort made to park, this time within the boundaries of the parking space.

It is unfair not to exercise care in parking, because one may through carelessness take two spaces instead of one and thus cause inconvenience to another person. A police officer may even give a driver a ticket for that.

The boundaries of a parking space tell one not to park anywhere and any way he or she pleases. There are rules to be followed. There are limits to one's liberty.

That is true of life. One cannot do anything he or she pleases. There are other people who have rights. They have feelings. They cannot be brushed aside as though they did not exist. Our freedom has its limits. There are boundaries of our existence. There are lines we are not to cross.

The Ten Commandments tell us about some of those lines. You have already learned about some of those commandments. You will be studying others as you grow older. It would be good to memorize them. They are worth knowing and keeping. One can never go wrong by doing right.

You have boundaries at home too. Some things go; others do not. We have our limits, and that is as it should be. I say, "Good for boundaries!"

# The Gift of Laughter

I am told that it requires many more muscles to frown that it does to smile. This means that it is easier to smile than it is to frown. But what about laughter? It must burn up a lot of energy to laugh, but it is about the best way to use energy that I know.

Some people almost never laugh. They don't see much that they think is funny. When other people are laughing, they may groan or keep a serious face. I was with a person once who laughed at things that she said but never at anything that anybody else said. The rest of us thought that what we said was funnier than what she said!

I feel sorry for people who can't laugh or who won't laugh. They miss a lot of fun.

Laughter is a gift. It is a way that God has created to help us enjoy ourselves and to help entertain others. Laughter is contagious. Let something funny happen or be told, and the laughter of one person kicks off a chain reaction. Before you know it, the whole group of people is laughing. I have one friend who holds himself around the middle when he laughs. I may be amused already, but I laugh even harder when I watch him.

There is much bad news in the world. Sorrow comes sooner than many of us are looking for it. Demanding times that do not allow for much laughter come to all of us. Many events that could cause tears are not very far away. Life and health and good fortune are uncertain. We should laugh when we can.

There is nothing merrier than the laugh of a child. So cheer the world up with a bright face, a sweet smile, and, best of all, a laugh that makes others happy.

# Our Teachable Dog

I want to tell you about a dog that our family once had. He was a beagle. A beagle is cut low to the ground with long, floppy ears. Do you know what we named our beagle? We named him Bugle — Bugle the beagle!

Bugle was about the cutest dog you would want to see. He wagged his tail almost constantly. He was black and brown and white with bright, cheerful eyes. He stayed so excited about living that he panted nearly all the time.

Bugle loved to do tricks. He was a very teachable dog. When he was a puppy he learned to play with a tennis ball. We would throw it a short way, and he would run after it. He learned to pick it up and bring it to us. Then we would throw it a little farther, and he would bring it back. Finally, we could throw it as hard as we could across the yard, and he would scamper away to find, pick it up, and come proudly back with his mouth full of ball!

Then we taught him to bark before we threw the ball. We would say, "Ball!" Bugle would give a long beagle bark. Then we would throw the ball. That was great fun for him and for us.

Then we taught him to bring in the paper from the front yard in the mornings. He would get hold of the paper very carefully right in the center to be sure he had it balanced so that he could run with it. He would then take off and bring it to us. We would pat him and talk to him and reward him by petting him. He would be so pleased with himself.

God has many things to teach us. I wish we could always be as eager to learn what God wants us to know as our little Bugle was to learn what we wanted to teach him. God wants to teach us about love and being helpful to our parents and kind to older people and unselfish with our brothers and sisters. When we learn some of those things, we will be as happy as Bugle was when he learned to bring in the paper.

# Pushing and Shoving Won't Do It

When you have been at a crowded football game or at a theater where there were many people, you may have been pushed by a person who wouldn't wait to get in or out. People were shoving past everybody who stood between them and where they wanted to go.

Such action is very rude. It does not respect the position and rights of others. To shove people aside is to say that they are not important enough to be dealt with as persons. I hope that you can always manage to wait your turn.

Pushing and shoving not only take place where bodies are jostled around; such also happens in other areas of life. You would know what someone meant if he or she said of another person, "I wish he would stop trying to push me around." Maybe it is a selfish individual who wants his way and who has chosen a poor way to try to get it done. That kind of approach to life will not work. It is sad to see people try to use it. I say it won't work because whatever persons do that treats others with lack of respect is not only ill-mannered but also against God's will.

We are made in the image of God. We are his children. He loves each one very much. He wills that we should live together with one another in our thoughts.

It isn't any fun to be pushed around. Don't be a pusher! Think about younger brothers and sisters at home, and don't take advantage of them because you are older and stronger. They have their own feelings and rights as you and I do. It is always good to remember the golden rule: Do to others as you would have them do to you.

# Reminders

A person in conversation may say, "That reminds me." What someone else says may remind one of some happening in the past or something that one intended to do. Sometimes reminders are sad, because they bring back thoughts of illness or disappointment or death. Often reminders are happy. They are good news, because they help us think again about people we love and grand times that we have had.

Not only are experiences reminders, but objects are as well. Think about two objects that belong to me. One is a little pocket knife that a friend gave me. I have frequent uses for that knife. I seldom bring it out of my pocket but what I think about him. He was a member of a church that I served, and we became friends for life. He crosses my mind many times, and the knife is a reminder of that friendship.

The second object is a watch that my children gave me. That watch makes me aware of the passing of time and that I should make the best use of it. In addition to that, it reminds me of those girls and of the love that we have always had for one another. Many times during the course of a busy day, I look at my watch to see what time it is. I not only become aware of the time, but my thoughts also take a quick trip to those precious people. Once they were little. Now they are grown. When I think of them, I am reminded of things that happened all along the way from the time they were babies to the present.

As you grow older, you will have experiences that remind you of other experiences, and you will collect some things that will make you think about people who are dear to you. These are good, because they keep us from forgetting to remember!

# Caring Children

What do you care about most? Some people care about themselves, what they can get others to do for them, what they can get out of doing something for others. They care about their clothes, their money, and having their way in all things. Theirs is a selfish life.

But what do you care about? Here are some things to think about.

You can care for your home. Homes vary in size. Some families have two parents; others, only one. Some homes have one child, and others have two or more. A home can be happy no matter what its size if its members are caring people. To think about the other people who live there and to do things that make them contented and happy are things that adults and children can do.

You can care about your schoolwork if you are old enough to be in school. The grades you make are important, but what you learn is the real issue. School is for learning. To care about that will help you become a good student, a person who appreciates knowledge.

You can care about your friends. Friendship is worth caring about. To take care not to misuse a friendship or to treat it carelessly is something every person should do. We come to feel even closer to a friend when we say nice things to or about that person. When we try to think what we can do to make that person aware of how much we think of him or her, the friendship deepens.

You can care about your church. To have the chance to grow up in a congregation that thinks a lot of children and youth is good fortune. Happy memories can develop in a caring church as you are a caring person in it.

Be careful what you think and what you love; then give yourself to the best that you know.

# What Do You Do When You Fall Down?

What do you do when you fall down? Children are so active that they frequently take tumbles. Sometimes clumsy adults stumble over things or lose their balance and fall. We will let the grown people settle with themselves what they are to do in such situations, and we will think about you.

If it hurts rather badly when you fall, you may cry. There is nothing wrong with that. Your skinned knee says to your mind, "I hurt." The mind says to the tears, "Do something about it. Cry." And so there come the tears. That can help for a little while, but that stage of the hurt should soon pass.

Have you ever seen someone keep on crying after the pain has passed in order to attract attention and get sympathy? That is when crying is not good. Even after people are grown, some of them still cry to get the attention and sympathy of people.

When you fall down you may get angry. If someone pushes you down, you may become angry with that person. If nobody else did it, you may get angry with yourself. It is as easy or easier to lose patience with ourselves as with other people. That kind of anger does us no good unless it helps us be more careful the next time.

When you fall down, the best thing to do is to get up.

Life gives us some hard times. Sometimes we give them to ourselves. To learn to get up is a great art. To want sympathy or to spend energy in anger is of little use. Get up! Don't wait for somebody to come along to pick you up. Get up! You will like yourself far better that way, and other people will as well.

# An Act to Remember

The Bible tells us that Jesus did something for his disciples on their last night together that might seem strange to you. He washed their feet. While they were at supper, he took a basin of water and a towel and went from one to the other, washing their feet. Why did he do that?

In those times people walked everywhere they went. There were no planes, trains, cars, or motorcycles. Maybe there was an occasional cart. Jesus walked to almost every place he went. The roads were hot and dusty. People wore sandals, which were not much protection from the dust or from the heat. After walking some distance, they would be ready for anything that would cool and refresh them. One sign that a person was glad that another person had come to visit was to have a servant wash the hot, dusty feet of the guest when he or she arrived. It was a sign of hospitality, of greeting, like our handshake. If there was no servant, the host did it.

On this night when Jesus and his twelve disciples were together for their last supper, there was no servant to wash the feet of those who were there. Jesus may have waited a few moments to see whether any of the disciples would offer to take the place of a servant and wash the feet of the others. They probably looked at one another and wondered who would volunteer. Nobody did.

So Jesus took the water and a towel and began to wash their feet as a servant would do. Then they became ashamed. One of them refused at first to let him do it. Jesus insisted, and he finally agreed. It must have been a tense time. All of them were too full of pride to do this act of courtesy and kindness for the others. When Jesus began to do it, they were embarrassed.

Times have changed. We ride in cars, and we wear shoes, and we do not wash the feet of our guests when they arrive. But the message is still there. We are not to be high and mighty. We are not to be full of pride and to think of ourselves as better than other persons. Christians are called to be servants of one another and of the world. We are to be humble and loving, caring for one another.